Before It Vanishes

10-27-90

To Leslie & David,
   I hope this bundle
of poems & sweets tickles
your fancy & tastes,
encourages your exploratory
yearnings, and delivers
you to our doorstep.
      Love,
      Allan
   802-748-9080.

Previous Books of Poetry by Robert Pack

The Irony of Joy
A Stranger's Privilege
Guarded by Women
Home from the Cemetery
Nothing but Light
Keeping Watch
Waking to My Name: New and Selected Poems
Faces in a Single Tree: A Cycle of Monologues
Clayfeld Rejoices, Clayfeld Laments: A Sequence of Poems

POETRY FOR CHILDREN
The Forgotten Secret
Then What Did You Do?
How to Catch a Crocodile
The Octopus Who Wanted to Juggle

Before It Vanishes

A PACKET FOR PROFESSOR PAGELS

by Robert Pack

DAVID R. GODINE
Publisher · Boston

The author wishes to thank the editors of the following magazines in which the poems in this collection first appeared: *The American Scholar, The Cream City Review, The Georgia Review, Green Mountains Review, Hampden-Sydney Review, The Kenyon Review, Michigan Quarterly Review, Middlebury Alumni Magazine, The New Criterion, The New England Review/Bread Loaf Quarterly, Poet and Critic, Poetry, Poetry Miscellany, Prairie Schooner, Quarterly West, Salmagundi, The Whole Earth Review.*

First edition published in 1989 by
David R. Godine, Publisher, Inc.
Horticultural Hall
300 Massachusetts Avenue
Boston, Massachusetts 02115

Library of Congress Catalogue Card Number: 89-45389
ISBN 0-87923-810-0 HC
ISBN 0-87923-813-5 SC

First edition
Printed in the United States of America

Contents

What if the sun
Be Centre to the World, and other Stars
By his attractive virtue and their own
Incited, dance about him various rounds?

— JOHN MILTON

Foreword

This cycle of poems was begun several years ago after I read Heinz R. Pagels's *The Cosmic Code*. I called Professor Pagels at the New York Academy of Science to explain the organization of my book to him and ask permission to quote from his book. I told him that in my poems he becomes my guide on a tour through the universe and that as a fictive character he changes identities, appearing sometimes as my friend, my father, son, or brother. His reply delighted me at the time: "That's good. I have a better chance of surviving as a fictive character than as a real one." The penultimate poem in the book, "The First Word at Last," was intended to be the concluding one; it was written in time for a reading I gave at the Reality Club in New York, which Heinz Pagels attended. Our personal friendship followed from that occasion. After his death in a climbing accident in 1988, I added "Outlasting You" as the final poem for this book, dedicated to his memory.

Stepping Out

If we could step outside the Milky Way, we could see that it is an immense spiral disk, its diffuse arms twisting around a central bulge of stars within which hides the galaxy's mysterious nucleus. . . . We see that the arms are delineated by bright blue stars and contain lots of dust and gas concentrating in star-forming nebulae. Our own sun is located on the inner edge of one such arm, the Orion arm. . . . Burning away hydrogen in their cores, cooking up helium, [stars] sing and vibrate for billions of years. . . . Eventually the sun will turn into a red giant and then into a white dwarf.

H E I N Z R . P A G E L S, *Perfect Symmetry*

All right, let's go, Professor Pagels,
       but I'll want to stay
a step behind you since that's not home turf for me
    out there—outside the Milky Way,

beyond the borders of beloved Vermont,
      even beyond the rocky coast
of Camden Harbor, Maine, where boyishly I watched
      returning fishing boats

    haul in their lobster catch in boxes
clustered with a mess of tails and claws,
      and wished the mind could spell itself
        a while from its own laws

without disturbing Nature. Now I stroll
      with you in space to see
that twisting spiral disk of gas and dust whose arms
      contain evolving nebulae;

I

to gaze, meandering, upon the bulge
of bright blue stars that hide
the still elusive nucleus
of our own galaxy. And there inside

Orion's arm is our own sun—
an ordinary star, except to us;
from here, beyond the Milky Way,
we see her as she was

all those light years away, ago,
as if, preserved within the mind, her past
were now, her spectral waves
embracing us, although, at last,

the fiery news of her distension—
death for earthlings—might
be speeding here upon its way.
Can we, aloft in thought's consoling flight,

return in time to warn them,
saying: Take one quick, concluding look out far
where—sword in hand—Orion
stares at Taurus, and our sun, our mother star,

no maiden like the Pleiades,
must undergo her fated change and swell
into a giant, like
bloated red Betelgeuse, who also will

decay to a white dwarf
shining with its last reserves of energy.
Earthlings, it isn't personal,
forget it's you whose lives must cease to be,

2

then the vibrating night
looms more magnificent to muse upon; forget—
as if you lived only in thought
forever fixed in what you see. And yet

our sun, Professor Pagels, homesick,
how I'll miss our sun, to her
let constellations sing—then on, my friend, lead on
to neighboring Andromeda.

Big Bang

*The present view of the creation, the "standard Big Bang model,"
maintains that the entire universe originated in an enormous explosion.
All matter was once concentrated into a very confined region in a
primordial matter soup. This matter soup expanded rapidly—it exploded.
In so doing it cooled down, enabling nuclei, then atoms, and finally
much later galaxies, stars, and planets to condense out of it. This
explosion is still going on today.*

HEINZ R. PAGELS, *The Cosmic Code*

If I had been, in the beginning, God
        brooding upon absence,
I might have pondered that if matter could be snatched
    from emptiness in an immense

        explosion, then allowed,
    with its expanding space, to cool—
        yes, that's the way to father
forth a universe! According to the rule

    (My favorite) of *entropy*
increase, I'd make time irreversible,
        measure it out, enabling
nuclei, then atoms, galaxies—the full,

        harmonious display
of stars and planets to condense into
        existence, always changing,
always entertaining Me with something new.

    And scattered randomly throughout
My galaxies, conditions surely would occur
        for oxygen and carbon
to combine, under an ordinary star, to stir

        inert cells to divide
and replicate themselves, and live, until
        evolving consciousness reveals
My thoughts as children who can share the thrill

        of watching, bud by bud by leaf,
                sweet fruitful things unfold
and be—and be replaced in shifts of light
        from green to red, from green to gold,

and red consumed in flourishing decay.
        I worry that their mortal wish
                for life to last will ruin
their moment of abundance in life's feast. . . . Relish

        it all, My sons, with eyes, with ears;
savor all songful matter with your tongue,
                like soup, with zestful words,
        and, while the universe is young—

just fifteen billion years, though colder now
                than when it was begun
blazing in hundred billions of degrees—
        this is *your* moment in the sun,

                a household star. Love her,
add laughter of your own to what you see:
        describe her as a grazing cow
across a field, perhaps a pollinating bee,

                who scents the blossoms
lifting upwind on the wafted air.
        Name her, Dolores, when she frowns
on cloudy afternoons, or when her hair

is loose like flowing wheat,
praise her clear radiance and call her Grace;
don't let your knowledge—she
cannot remain—mar your approval of her face.

And you, Professor Pagels,
you will serve as My new representative;
of all the holy names I've had,
Big Bang is raunchy good as any you can give

with My original
explosion, lo! still going on today. . . .
But please remind your rhyming friend
that even laughing fathers pass away.

Pepper and Salt

To illustrate entropy increase, take a glass jar and fill it up a quarter of the way with salt. Then add granulated pepper until it is half full. There is a black layer on top of a white layer—an improbable configuration of all the particles. . . . Now shake the jar vigorously. The result is a gray mixture, a disorganized configuration of the salt and pepper. If you keep shaking, it is very unlikely that the original configuration will ever return. Not in a million years of shaking will it return.

HEINZ R. PAGELS, *The Cosmic Code*

With just two shakes of the glass jar—voilà!
       the scattered pepper
    organizes to the top;
salt burrows underneath. A blurred

    reflection of its crystal whiteness
merges with the oak grain on the oval table
      by the east-view window where I sit.
        One daffodil

    is leaning from a glazed, green vase;
      it shimmers moistly
though I cut it days ago, nor is there
      change of heart in me,

    watching the cow-faced sun lift up
      her head to graze
over the hazy mountains
twenty miles away. Shadows of pear trees

    leap across the lawn now sparkling
      with the beaded dew;
a phoebe dips her tail and darts off
      toward the nest she built two years ago.

My sleeping father,
visiting my house, is dreaming he
has come back to the farm where he was born;
I think that he can see

his father lacing his own work boots on.
Surely the coffee's taste is true,
surely the lemon light across the hills
right now, and also you,

Professor Pagels, in my mind,
doffing the cap my own son wears when gardening,
convinced that entropy does not apply
to my imagining

the dawn sun is a cosmic cow,
who utterly consumes the rough cud of the world
to nourish nature in return
with no milk spilled

the trees do not lap up. No light is lost
when my benign command—*Let be*—
restores the salt-and-pepper table still life
of invented memory

with you, as my companion,
hoe and rake in hand, impatient there
to help me weed the garden
as the melancholy morning air

softly disperses
its gold hue on tilled soil patterned into rows.
And now, across the plotted fields,
actual cows,

miniature as ivories,
look up to see the flow of bordered green
             contained. I shake the jar
again to get on with my life—the scene

             changes to salt specks flying;
dandelion fuzz whirls with the windy day;
             exploding or collapsing stars
recede forever through the Milky Way.

Come with me now to tend the garden;
yes, my rakish son, come hoe along with me,
             and we'll compose from dust
a round of ordered entropy.

After All

After the first tenth of a second had passed, the universe cooled down to about ten billion degrees Kelvin. . . . All that remained was electrons, neutrinos, and photons. After three minutes had passed . . . the particles were less agitated [and] the small contamination of protons and neutrons [could] combine into nuclei. . . . Only after about a hundred thousand years had elapsed did the temperature drop sufficiently for the electrons to combine with the nuclei to form atoms. . . . After a few billion years, the universe began to look as it presently does.

H E I N Z R . P A G E L S, *The Cosmic Code*

I can recall my father telling me,
          while putting me to bed,
the story of God's first six days of work,
          before He rested, when He said:

"Let there be light," and, after He divided
          waters of the deep with firmament,
"Let the dry land appear," was His command.
          I knew exactly what God meant

when He gave orders—things got done—unlike
          my father's threats to me
that I had damn well better stop
pinching my brother. My dad couldn't see

          that was impossible:
so many pinchings back and forth required
          two pinches more. In one way, though,
I knew they were alike: God never tired

of saying certain words—"And let
the earth bring forth," when summoning the grass,
            or, when He made the stars—
"And let them be for signs." Dad couldn't pass

        over those "lets" without a rumble
in his voice, and then, for emphasis, each time
            "God saw that it was good"
came back, he'd jump up from my bed, and climb

        the box where my best toys were kept,
and launch his words out, rolling in the lull
            that marked the stages of God's work.
The word "good" seemed too tame to me; "sensational"

            is what I would have said,
"God saw it was sensational," the most
            complete world He could make;
maybe, I thought, God didn't want to boast,

            and, anyway, sensational
sounds funny to repeat, unlike plain "good."
            The fifth day was my favorite
            because I understood—

as if we shared a secret—why the Lord
        liked whales: they're big *and* friendly, though
they aren't fish, they're mammals—*that* is something,
        I believed, a God should know.

        Whales were the only creatures
God Himself had named; He should have made
        them on the same day He made men.
            Because I'm still afraid

to let go in the dark, to sleep,
without a lullabying story saying how
        the universe began,
        Professor Pagels, tell me now,

in fractions, minutes, eons, and degrees,
        like God's six working days,
so I can memorize them for *my* son,
        the stages I can name and praise

through fifteen billion years of space expanding
        like a pebble's ripples in a pool:
After the first tenth of a second passed,
        the universe commenced to cool;

        God saw that it was good,
and after just three minutes had gone by,
        less agitated then,
protons and neutrons merged as nuclei;

        and only after a brief
hundred thousand years, electrons could combine
        with nuclei—and thus
were atoms formed. "This universe of Mine

        is good, damned good, and some might say
My work's sensational," said God. And so it was
        that after a few billion years
our world began to look as presently it does—

        though when we've finished killing
off His whales, when no one living can recall,
        what story of us will be told
if He is there to tell it, after all?

Proton Decay

Most visible matter—stars, galaxies, and gas clouds—is made of hydrogen, and the nucleus of the hydrogen atom is a single proton. If protons decay, then the very substance of the universe is slowly rotting away like a cancer that infects matter itself. This rotting away of matter will, according to these unified [field] theories, take about a thousand billion billion (10^{21}) times the present age of the universe. We will have lots of time to explore the universe before it vanishes.

H E I N Z R. P A G E L S, *The Cosmic Code*

From where I stand, Professor Pagels,
pausing in the tall grass as I climb the pathless hill
    back to my house, picking wild asters for
        the red vase on my window sill,

    I say to you out loud *how much*—
how much I wish to dwell within the dwindling harvest
    of my life a longer while,
    how much our universe is blessed

        simply by being here,
where nothing might have been, with still to go some
    thousand billion billion times the age
    we have already come

if matter is infected with such cancerous
    but slow proton decay.
I greet your greeting to explore our universe
    before time radiates away,

    although, Professor, stranger, your
field theory estimate of crabbing time's disease
    stretches the earthbound scale
of my mere mankind-measuring anxieties.

And yet I know that my wild asters
from the umbering, September valley hold
        their glow for three days
in my house, their yellow centers tarnish into gold—

        then they're forever gone,
partaking of disaster matter must at last
        experience. Right now there are
more species than *this* griever in the parting grass

        can keep at heart, in mind,
like Aromatic, Bushy, Calico, with purple blue,
        and through the alphabet to Showy,
Upland White, and Willow, my thought-gifts to you,

        my fellow mourner. So, let us
        be bound by flowing grace
of words that cherish, words that touch across
        what mortal time and space

remain, though even if we two could live to name
        each single flower and each leaf,
those billions of last years before the end
        would seem too sad, too brief,

        when, inescapably, the end did come.
Always, in thought, the end nears now—death in our minds
        outlives our lives, it's part of us,
it's always what our wakeful searching finds,

        and every flowered star we love
        is brief as azure nightfall on this hill,
brief as companionable breath that lengthens into words
        and then goes still.

Place

I could be kneeling in my garden on
            a planet with the name
of Earth, but in another galaxy.
        Each bean, each squash could be the same

as they are here, though billions of light years
            from our own Milky Way.
I could be circling through the autumn light
        on any undistinguished day,

within a solar system that evolved
        according to no special rules,
allowing life to organize itself
            from protein molecules,

laughing at nothing in particular.
            I'd laugh out loud because
    just being in no special place,
yet being there alive with time to pause

        and words upon my tongue
enabling me to measure out that pause as such
        and thus possess my pausing self
            (as if my mind could touch

its wild reflection in the splattered shade)
    seemed all the cause laughter required.
I'd hold a glossy eggplant at arm's length
    to contemplate its shape, inspired

        by my composing eye,
    which sees its swelling hue repeat
·the sunset purple from the distant hills,
        so that I feel complete

        control an instant, balancing
    the fertile darkness at my fingertips,
        darkness made visible, as if
            before my moistened lips

        boldly pronounced its solid name,
    I was the center of the universe,
            as if my eggplant were
    the quintessential fruit, for better or for worse

        till death, the model after which
    (platonic absolute beyond mere human sense!)
            succeeding eggplants scattered
    out among the stars would be just variants.

        My one sufficient privilege
    would be invented freedom from fixed circumstance
        through laughing words, through music
    patterned beyond randomness and chance,

        music of what we improvise
    to keep ourselves revolving in our place,
            our temporary world
        of ordinary, curving space.

Let's call this now distinguished world our home,
    wherever we may be;
this legendary eggplant will provide the bond
    that makes of laughter, company.

Neanderthal Poem Ah *Number One*

Although one letter "a" is identical to another "a", words and
sentences can be different. . . . Likewise, in our universe there are only a
few fundamental building blocks: quarks, leptons, and gluons. These are
the letters of the alphabet of nature. With this rather small alphabet,
words are made—these are atoms. The words are strung together, with
their own special grammar—the laws of quantum theory—to form
sentences, which are molecules. Soon we have books, entire libraries, made
out of molecular "sentences." . . . Out of identity came difference.

HEINZ R. PAGELS, *The Cosmic Code*

Leaping leptons, gluons, and quarks—
    difference from identity!
Sound me the *a*, Professor Pagels, from your name,
    sound me a *b*;

    ra! ra! we've started, now a *c*,
        ca—abracadabra;
dance me the prestidigitation of the alphabet
    back to an *a* released as *ah!*

ah as in qu*a*rk: and thus an *a*, conjoined
            with *ah*, prolonged and rounded,
    might have been the primal word
        for joy unbounded

from astonished ape-like lips—an *ah*, an *ahr*,
        resounding from the lungs,
    reverberating *hahr* up to the teeth,
        until the tongue,

discovering a purpose to its taste,
     plucked teasing, consonantal *t*,
          and thus gave shape to *heart*,
atomic word for the anatomy

     of art, for speech, *ah* yes, delighting
          in its parts. Words are a lake
in which we look, Professor, partner, at
     ourselves, reflecting what we make,

as morning brightens crimson in the mist,
          from what we hear and see—
     a rondo of frogs rumbling,
light wind lilting lento in the willow tree.

     Such mimic long *o* wind-words
bind us over silent distances, although
     we two, in fact, have never met;
          and yet in thought I go

with you where, glowing gluons, your thoughts go.
          So if you read these
     *ah*s, these *oh*s, this cry of origins,
          call of identities,

     perhaps you'll follow me over
the glade, over the clover-purple hill,
     where once my father led me—I
          can see him still—

to find the spring that starts the minnow stream
     that sloshes pebbles burbling
through the pendant, orange jewelweed,
          then bubbles loudly, merging

with the courting bullfrog bellows echoed
    in the cattail marshes all
along the margins of the lake. There you can hear
    the world's first bard Neanderthal

bleat out an *a* into an *ah!* And *oh*,
    Professor Pagels, *ah* and *oo*,
across the separating spaces now,
    from you to me and me to you,

        molecular sentences flow
connecting differentiated strangers, *oo!* Trees
    bloom with leaves of words; *oh*s blow
from the low lake to cool entire libraries.

Intending Words

*Increase in entropy [measures] the change of a closed physical system
from a configuration with relatively low probability to one with high
probability. . . . When gas [in a container filled with two different
gases] reaches a state of maximum entropy—that is, particles are
thoroughly mixed and maximally messy—it is said to be in an
"equilibrium state." There is nothing you can do to increase its
messiness; hence it is in equilibrium, achieving the stability of complete
disorder.*

H E I N Z R . P A G E L S, *Perfect Symmetry*

Again your words help me
invoke *my* Muse, Professor Pagels—messiness,
        though not yet maximal, indeed,
is what I contemplate, I must confess,

        surveying what my words have reaped,
watching November rain, while dusk descends,
        make luminous the marred
and unpicked apples. Lady Entropy now rends

        the pulpy late fruit down to rot,
                to feed the nuzzling deer
before snow suffocates the mealy grass.
        It's not harvesting death I fear

        so much as my own lurking
headlong wish for easeful equilibrium
        that undermines my autumn effort
to hold on. Silence should be my medium,

more probable than speech,
since measured bounty—apples tended on a tree
    like verbs on my pursed lips—
burdens my thoughts with sighs from Lady Entropy

    not to resist the urge
toward stable messiness—wordless disorder past
    which nothing can get messier.
My Lady's lullabying voice at last

    persuades me, saying: "See my apples
    squandered on the ground;
I cherish them, but form is so improbable,
    since always particles are found

dispersing to be uniformly messy, I must let
    unstable life decay." Yet now,
aroused, I tell her: "Doubtful words at least can bless
    each apple on its bough;

the network silhouette of black, wet twigs
    against a silver haze
of drizzling sky; patterns of hoofprints faintly
    circling in the windy maze

of whirling leaves." And now, Professor, look!
    through settled mist, a glow
of golden tamaracks prolongs the light, as if
    my Lady, too, reluctant to let go,

    composed one more design,
one more improbable tableau, to hold in sight
    with rainy words intending to
express some purpose yearning matter might

yet yield if I could father form
        in her forlorn embrace.
There are no stars tonight, no haloed moon;
        I improvise her face

        from what the undivided dark allows.
This windless moment she lies down with me,
        whispers one soothing hymn
of one unlikely apple hanging on a tree.

Quantum Weirdness

At last you physicists have verified
    that matter's indeterminate.
My freedom-seeking soul suspected so,
    but now a worldly weight

    is lifted from my mind: electrons—
        you have liberated me
to understand, Professor Pagels—can't be measured
    for position and velocity

at once. They're like—and here's the rub—they're like
    my wife! When she is out of sight
she's focused in my memory, but when
    she's standing here and right

before my eyes, she blurs, her whirling presence
    overwhelms me with her presentness.
"Is she *observer-created*, and thus a jumble
    of my own projected guesses,

out of need?" I mumble to myself,
then, basso profundo, broadly to her:
        "Thy cheeks are as a snowfall
        in a field where no winds stir;

thy hair is as the murmuring of pines
        at twilight in the scented haze
                as, pausing with her fawn,
the round-eyed doe beside the stream grazes

        as if I almost might
compose her in a permanence of grace
        where place is immanent with movement,
                movement settles into place."

        "Do you mean me?" she asks askance.
"Or are you in the quantum world again,
        conjuring quarks with Herr Professor,
        your imaginary friend?"

What metaphor can measure her or hold her
                unpredictably in mind?
How can elusiveness be cherished, touched,
        if body cannot be defined

by where it is? I never find her wholly
                where she seems to be,
so, use your influence, my connoisseur
        of weirdness, intercede for me

to tell her she appears in Gilead as I
        behold her vanishing from view;
tell her: "Thine hands touch everywhere at once
        like autumn dew."

Table, Chair, Cat

*[Quantum theory of the atomic world] requires a definite line between
the observed and the observer, a split between object and mind
. . . it does not not say where the line between them is drawn. The
microworld lacks standard objectivity. But should this weirdness get out
into the ordinary world of tables, chairs, and cats?*

H E I N Z R . P A G E L S, *The Cosmic Code*

The cat upon the table, snoozing
by the bowl of oranges, is not aware
    I'm watching her across a line
between observer and observed that must be there

       in the atomic world;
she's free to sleep an ordinary sleep
    in which a cat is just a cat.
Father of thought, Professor Pagels, you can't keep

    your knowledge of the microworld
from getting out in my own living room,
    now that you've sown it in my head,
       now that my mind, this womb

each fresh idea can fertilize, conceives
       of leptons, gluons, quarks—
configurations of atomic particles,
    leftover remnants from the dark,

dense, Big Bang superhot beginning—we
    inherit and are fashioned from.
Is there a line as well that separates the mind
       from its own self? Oh, come!

paternal, quantum ghost, come sit by me
    in this embellished, quantum chair,
        where evenings by the fire
my father sat spellbound in thought. I'd stare

    at his unfathomable face,
but there was nothing he would say to me;
        I don't know what I hoped for—
something pushed our bond apart, but I could see

    it wasn't personal, although
he'd stroke my sleeping arm as he walked by
        as if it were a cat. I can
            remember how I'd try,

by squinting hard, to watch the table move
    within itself, its molecules
bumping, unwilling to stay still, and yet
        obeying table rules,

content to be what any table is,
    with four straight chairs for company.
I think I changed my father, and I'm roused
        to think that he changed me,

just by our looking at each other. No,
    we're not free not to think—that's weird,
Professor, weirdly true, and freely I
        admit it, though you fear

weirdness would split our ordinary world.
        Look there! Can you see that—
that far light on the oranges? This poem,
    my friend, is bound to wake my cat!

The Invisible Hand

*The best place to look for chaos is right in the atom. Although
individual random events [are] meaningless, the distribution of those
events . . . could be the subject of an exact science—probability theory.
. . . What is perceived as freedom by the individual is thus necessity from
a collective viewpoint. The die when it is thrown may "think" it has
freedom, but . . . it is part of a probability distribution; it is being
influenced by the invisible hand.*

HEINZ R. PAGELS, *The Cosmic Code*

I've never had much trouble finding chaos
    even in the macroworld
of tables, chairs, and cats—and specially
        of kids. For sure, they're hurled

about by random energy, and all
    a parent knows is: *move they must*!
Intention hardly matters, so hi-ho they're off—
    bumped atoms in a cloud of dust.

    When doing what their bodies
burn to do, thoughtless, they feel they're free,
    while quantum theory says
dice-throwing probability,

    fate's hand, determines with
a seven or a snake-eyes toss
the distribution of who wins and who craps out,
    but not the consciousness of loss,

which means only what I assign to it.
    When I was eight or nine
at camp, returning from an all-day hike,
    scratched and fatigued, I fell behind,

unnoticed by my bunk mate and my counselor.
　　I shoved aside a rotted log
to look for salamanders or a spotted newt,
　　　　listened for a wood frog

to add to my collection, when I saw
　　　　half-shaded from the sun,
　　curled tightly amid packed-down leaves,
　　a snake, the very one

　　I recognized from last year's hike,
but I had failed to catch. Ah, I was faster now;
　　　　I felt fresh power surge
in my crouched legs; I paused, for I knew how

　　　　to mesmerize him with a stare.
He sensed my body's heat with his quick tongue—
　　　　and tried to slither sideways
out of reach, but like a spear, I flung

　　　　myself at him, grabbed him
around the middle as uncoiled alarm
　　　　writhed in my tightened squeeze
and shuddered through the muscles in my arm,

　　　　into my shoulders and my back.
One thrust, and swifter than a shooting star,
　　　　I stuffed him in my lunch pail
with my half-remaining candy bar,

　　　　my compass, and my knife.
　　When we got back to camp, instead
of praising me for what I'd done, my counselor screamed,
　　　　"You dumb kid, that's a copperhead!

Look at those hourglass markings!
Don't you ever take a chance like that again!"
He glared at me—I swear his eyes
turned glassy-black, just like the snake's—and then

he slapped me on the mouth.
I felt the chaos of his blow
explode improbably upon my lips.
I did not duck; I was too slow

even to see it coming—blam!—as if
his hand had been invisible.
Now I'm determined that his influence, which my
own chosen parable

makes manifest, receives wide distribution; thus
let snake-eyes represent the soul
of science laughingly set free—a sign of luck.
OK, Professor? It's *your* roll.

Are Quarks the End?

*It would take an infinite amount of energy to pull two quarks apart.
Since an infinite amount of energy is not available, quarks cannot be
separated. . . . Are quarks the end of the road? Or are quarks themselves
made out of more fundamental objects? . . . All present evidence supports
this view that quarks are a "rock bottom" to matter, but no physicist I
know would be willing to bet much on that.*

H E I N Z   R.   P A G E L S, *The Cosmic Code*

Light years ago, carefree, I leapt
into the gambler's seat of fatherhood,
    quick with love's certain energy,
      before I understood

    the stakes I'd chipped in—to be lost?
Now, nearing my road's end, I've got to get
      back that first gambler's faith;
I feel the earthbound foxhole need to bet

    a fundamental bond
makes life, makes matter indivisible
    at some point that the finite mind
can comprehend. A willing mind can will

    itself at one with what it is
      composed of—as the son,
a father now himself, at last accepts
    his father's sorrow as his own.

"The story of my leaving started here," he thinks,
    standing beside the limestone gate
his agitated father built the day
      that, almost three weeks late,

he, finally, ass-backwards, choking, lucky
        to survive, was born.
    And now, his own son grown and gone,
he sees his striding father once again—though worn

    more at the corners of his eyes,
squinting, and flushed beneath his beaver hat
        from the subzero wind—
enter the glaring doorway, as the cat

        scoots out between his legs,
    his arms piled to his chin with wood
        split for the morning fire.
Or was that image fabricated as he stood

    a moment at the open door,
seeing the aura of himself, in frosty air,
        composed through his approving son's
            immortalizing stare?

Father and son, I see them merged, forever
    bound and circling in the mind,
        as if what matters is
        the utter otherness you find

within yourself without which you are lost
    to be your forlorn self alone!
Before you ante up, Professor Pagels, with
    your fellow physicists, your own

identifying kind, I'll play the father, soon
    to leave, thus free to speak his fears
        to you, his heeding son.
    Meet me, before the moon appears,

beside the gate my long-dead father built,
    to listen in the binding dark
for my best full-house blessing: "Place your bet
    on the rock-bottom quark."

Autumn Warmth

*The universe today [with its background-radiation temperature
measured to be 2.7 Kelvin] is the frozen remnant of the Big Bang. Like
an ice crystal that has frozen out of a uniform water vapor, it has lots of
structure—the galaxies, stars, and life itself. But according to the
modern view, even the protons and neutrons—the very substance of
matter— are the frozen fossils of the Big Bang. They too were created as
the temperature fell.*

HEINZ R. PAGELS, *Perfect Symmetry*

A fossil, yet I'm here, Professor Pagels,
    bare-armed in my garden, yanking out
        the wooden stakes supporting
my profuse tomato plants, now that the rout

        of robust weeds, twin triumph
with my bumper crop, has been concluded by
    the first October killing frost
        last night's unclouded sky

made unpreventable. Low morning sun
        softens the nestling air,
and, slowly, I absorb its bleak, mild rays.
    Hornets bore in the rotting pears

        clinging from loosened stems;
wasps in the spider-threaded eaves
        deliriously thrum,
as if their armored bodies must believe

        their harvest will not end. Shaken,
scraped clean, for next year's use, of clotted soil,
    the stakes go bundled to the shed;
the rototiller, drained of gas and oil,

hunches beside the hanging row
of shovels, hoes, and rakes, dreaming of upturned stones;
      a sluggish garter snake
slips past a silhouette of crushed toad bones.

    Along the stacked, dry boulder wall
that frames the sweep of my whole lawn, borders
      my garden, and asserts my place,
I pile leftover green tomatoes, pumpkins, gourds—

      my galaxy of vegetables—
as testimony that I lived here, too,
      with all my fellow fossils—
protons, neutrons, yes, and you,

Professor, whom I picture with a huge
      thermometer, rectal
of course (just like the one my mother used),
      still measuring the spectral

background radiation of the universe—
      a frozen remnant of
Big Bang whose one fireball creative secret,
      like a god's initiating love

embodied, merely was to let things cool.
    Now I can see along the margin
of the steady lake, the spreading aggregate
      of simple grains, the faint, thin

glaze of ice; and now, condensed, night's vapor
      on a shaded willow tree,
leaf after leaf, reveals its crystal hexagons—
      hint of the perfect symmetry

before the cosmic cooling started. Yet
       I know that too much cold
can uncreate created living form.
       Our season in the sun grows old,

            although there is enough
       warmth left at least to keep me awed
at my awareness of myself as remnant,
            gourd or green tomato, flawed

so lately into life—according to the clock
       of temperature decrease. As one
fossil to another, "Please put down your thermometer
       and join me in the sun!"

The Speck in the Soup

At the first hundreth of a second the temperature of the primordial soup was one hundred billion degrees Kelvin. The soup consisted mostly of electrons, positrons, photons, neutrinos, and antineutrinos. These particles were continually being created and destroyed as they interacted. . . . There was also a small contamination of protons and neutrons, and about one billionth the number of photons. . . . Out of that speck in the soup, all the galaxies and stars and ultimately the earth will be made.
H E I N Z R . P A G E L S, *The Cosmic Code*

Thank you, Big Bang, for that contamination of
        protons and neutrons. Oh!
without it—other particles destroyed
      through interaction—there'd be no

        material to make
a universe, no Milky Way
to mother us, no random planet, Earth,
      to call our home. Some bard might say—

        if, like you physicists,
he, too, had appetite enough to stoop
to use such yummy metaphors
      as *primordial soup*—

      "Without that speck no Alpha could
commence to tell its cosmic tale; some primal flaw
      is needed to cook up a plot."
        The necessary law

of storytelling is that something changes,
        something must go wrong.
    A bland broth it would be without
the legendary sorrows of uplifting song.

Applauding, satisfied Omega
knows that happiness
requires a death to measure out an end, define
our passing musically, and bless

our disappearance in a choir of praise.
Inherent laughter sang
itself out from the alphabet,
each letter there a fossil left by you, Big Bang,

cooling to suit your preference
for tangy speech—a zestful, piquant brew
of pungent words. Alphabet soup,
animal soup, aardvark to zebra, oo,

and then comes us, incarnate
and alive in breathing dust,
from imperfection, just a speck, sentenced
to speak, to sing, to trust

what laughter knows: that we must willingly
relinquish to the earth, our home,
the particles we borrow
that comprise a human body—ours, our own,

yet only for a while,
and only once, Professor Pagels, yours and mine,
never again to stand here awed
among this multitude of mortal stars, divine

unto ourselves. I savor, yum,
the soup of my flawed origin—and now I live
to taste my portion on my lips,
Oh cosmic yum, Oh yum definitive!

Recipe

Each plant depends upon an ecological network; likewise, with planets, stars, and galaxies. . . . The atoms of planets and the atoms in our bodies consist of many heavy chemical elements that were cooked up out of lighter elements in the nuclear furnaces of stars long ago. . . . Like life in a garden, life in the universe depends on a complex relation of parts to the whole.

H E I N Z   R .   P A G E L S, *Perfect Symmetry*

That's food for thought, since it appears our chef,
　　Big Bang, was able to contrive,
　　　　billions of years ago,
a recipe for atoms that could come alive

　　because the furnaces of stars
cooked up each needed chemical ingredient.
　　Our universal soup-mixer's
　　　　original intent

moved him to cultivate a network garden
　　in which all things are related—you,
Professor Pagels, me, the plants and animals.
　　We're all in the same cosmic stew

　　　　together, one might say,
and easily digestible, I fear—
　　I mean the earth will swallow us,
breathing our atoms back into the atmosphere,

　　back to the planets, stars,
and galaxies that, like our bodies, all are made
　　from the same elements; and yet
we feast on our *own* lives in sun, in shade,

which we depend upon
for chlorophyll, for midday rest.
Each hungry cell partakes of the vast body
of the universe, and, at our best,

we know ourselves as one
self knowing one is but a particle,
part of a larger whole. Though just
a wink in dreamless time, still we are fully

conscious strands of molecules,
consumingly aware, down to the bone,
of our sweet self-taste on our tongues,
with pungent death at last to call our own.

To savor other selves, eating
our lovesick hearts out in devouring thought,
we seek the life surviving
for the owl when the blind mole is caught,

identifying with them both—
ongoing energy, ongoing death.
Eternal appetite—
the soul of body and of breath—

flashes its teeth in calcium and phosphorus
under the animating sun
by whose flames we must see our flames go out,
uniting each with everyone.

Let our lamenting minds desire this consummation
of dispersing light;
let rain descend unto our garden bed
like loosened weeping in the night.

Neutrinos

In spite of their enormous numbers, [neutrinos] do not contribute much to the total mass of the universe. But if they have mass, then it is estimated that they would account for 90 percent of all the mass of the universe—an invisible mass, because no one can actually see this neutrino "background radiation." The other 10 percent—the minor part—is the visible matter in the form of stars and galaxies. Neutrinos could thus account for the "missing mass"—the amount required to halt the expansion of the universe and cause it, finally, to contract.

H E I N Z R . P A G E L S , *The Cosmic Code*

This fall I'm rooting for contraction!
Please, Professor Pagels, find the missing mass
      that would assure mankind
expansion will reverse and bring to pass

      the ultimate collapse,
some distant but inevitable day,
      of matter on itself. I'd know
the universe would go its wished-for way

      returning to the nothing
it originated from; Big Bang would detonate
      space-time into existence
once again, and once again our fate

      would be a universe of gas
expanding into stars and galaxies.
      Such cycles breathing out
and breathing in—eternities

unto themselves—depend upon the gravity
of background radiation. Oh!
my happy, holiest of rounded hopes
is that invisible neutrinos

possess the needed mass
to keep the universe from thinning out forever
to a lifeless void, a bland,
undifferentiated cosmic mist, never

to be born again, never to fashion
suns and moons, rivers, forests, mountains, trees,
a planet tilted on its axis
for each season's sake (at twenty-three degrees),

migrating robins, crocuses,
red tulips, daffodils,
then summer lilies, honeysuckle, columbine
(how eagerly each sweet name trills

liltingly on the tongue to welcome them!)
and on to autumn when
the valley fills with aster, hyssop, goldenrod,
until first snow skips back again

and pale narcissus, sprouting inside by a window
in a blue, ceramic bowl,
unfold the bloom of their aroma in the dawn.
To love the universe, the whole

flowering pageant of emerging forms, always
has meant we've hoped for the return
of each leaf, permanent in paradise, and yet
I know that we must learn

recurrence can't restore what's *here*: moonlight
       bestowing stillness on my wife,
my sunlit daughter savoring a peach,
          my own remaining life.

Professor, if your blank neutrino does
         have any mass at all,
a tilted planet would fulfill my mortal wish
       for springtime, summer, winter, fall.

Let There Be Colored Light

The first 300,000 years was a burning universe of darkness, opaque to the transmission of light. . . . But once the temperature falls below 3,000 Kelvin, the electrons combine with the nuclei to form true atoms because the photons are no longer energetic enough to knock them apart. Now the photons . . . are free to fly about at the speed of light. All at once the universe becomes transparent, bathed in a brilliant yellow light. . . . The temperature continues dropping, and its color changes from yellow, to orange, to red, to deep red, and then to the darkness of deep space.

H E I N Z R . P A G E L S, *Perfect Symmetry*

Three hundred thousand opaque years
of burning darkness—then
a universe at once made visible, suffused
with light exactly when

true atoms form, a brilliant yellow light
of liberated photons, free
to give expanding space the sacred gift
of sumptuous transparency.

Thank you, Professor Pagels,
for informing me how, as the atoms cool,
the universal yellow changes
into orange deepening to red—a pool

in which a blazing god
might watch himself become incarnate, praised be He!,
through radiation waves
proportional inversely to their energy.

"Let there be wavelengths
undulating blue; let there be longer ones for red;
        let yellow mix with them," perhaps
            the Lord of photons said,

        may He be praised, having brought forth
the primal, necessary colors from
                which all the shades and hues,
        the infinite gradations, of all colors come.

Yellow to orange, red to deeper red, and now
            familiar darkness of deep space—
that's fifteen billion years of forms emerging
                like expressions on the face

of some unfathomable deity,
                some purposeful, vast mind,
        although I must admit to you
            my aching cannot find

solace for unrelenting death—my parents',
            children's, wife's, my own—
in fantasizing some redeeming god prefers us
                to a star, a tree, a stone.

Still in this unbelieving year, seasons
            return, and still to me returns
                day, blindly wishing
for more light, more colored light that burns

        by rousing my mind's last resource
in praising everything that flourishes to form.
            Praise to the strength that praise confers
upon the praiser who, content to warm

his hands at his own flame,
content to name himself, makes purposeful
his moment in our little sun,
makes purposeful his vanishing, the pull

back to the opaque dark
before the universe was bathed in yellow light.
Praise to the spectrum of the stars
receding in expanding space; praise to the night,

which helps us see their colors shift;
praise to the morning tree whose shimmered green
turns greener with reflecting dew;
and then let praise be seen

upon the dated marble where at length
one lays one's unenlightened head—
praise to residing sunset orange, glowing
visible to deepened red.

Recounting the Past to Come

*On the time scales of our universe, all our acts seem empty. It is as if
we had never existed. . . . The madness, the glory and joy of our species
are destined to an oblivion so complete that even the act of destruction
will not be remembered. . . . [But] no current cosmological model views
as important the effect on the future of the universe of intelligent life.
Perhaps life will influence the cosmos in an as-yet-unforeseen way.*

HEINZ R. PAGELS, *Perfect Symmetry*

Beholding spindrift rainbow haze and spume—
    peaked waves completing what they are—
my eyes contain their vanishing. The tide recedes
    at sunset as the evening star,

bright Venus, now ascends from the horizon
    in a breathless instant into view,
        throbbing as she absorbs
more red from vibrant twilight's purple blue—

    unlike my mind which disappears
into itself in thought's bleak aftermath.
        Out of my emptied light,
I lift myself to find the tangled path

    back to my cabin and my friend.
I pause to watch a late crow shifting on a post;
        weirdly, in moonlight, he
    appears immaculate, a ghost

        of lustered white, as if
he were the absence of himself, bereft
        yet visible, as if I saw him
in the place he had already left,

poignantly gone, so vivid
in a past that's yet to come, it seems to add
a gorgeous aura to the bird.
Then—with a raucous blast of caws, a mad,

ungainly scrambling of his wings,
fearful of God knows what, perhaps of me—
the glossy bird flaps out
into the kindred dark to find his tree.

My friend waits for me in our cabin,
baking bread; he breathes its smell to keep
some sweetness in his mind
before my hand will stab him in his sleep—

the dream he can't escape
because he needs to see himself as dead,
but through my eyes, be done with his
own dull, slow, daily dread

of unrelieved oblivion,
destruction so complete
that it will be as if he never lived
to feel the warm sand on his feet,

never enjoyed the shimmered hint of rainbow
glinting in the windfall haze.
And yet, through me, he will
survive himself, preserve the days

he walked home from the beach along our path;
by mourning him before he dies—
at one with what he minded, what he watched—
I see the crow before his eyes

turn moonlit white, dissolve,
become the lengthened presence of his vanishing.
        And when my friend gets to our cabin,
finds me lying there asleep, a ring

        of spectral light around my head,
his glare reflected on my dreaming face,
            he'll know this meeting of his mind
                    with his own death, gives place

        to blank oblivion, and lets
it influence his seeing what I must foresee.
            My friend withdraws his dagger
from my chest—I wake to my eternity

        to contemplate my future now
                as if it were my past,
to glory in this present absence of a wave
        even whose absence cannot last.

The Red Shift

for Ira and Linda Pastan

The discovery of the expansion of the universe [was made] by Edwin
Hubble in 1929–1931. He observed that the red shift of the light from
distant galaxies is proportional to their distance from us. His conclusion
is based on the fact that an atom which is moving away from us at high
velocity, such as in a distant galaxy, has its spectral lines shifted to the
red in proportion to its velocity.

HEINZ R. PAGELS, *The Cosmic Code*

I'll bet that Hubble made
his mind-bending discovery
by first observing in
himself a red shift in the galaxy

of his own past, watching the boy
who he once was recede
knee-deep across the bending grass
at hazy dawn where windblown roses breed

in scrubby patches by the cliff.
He sees him carrying a bright red pail
to put collected seashells in
as he descends, holding the driftwood rail

his father made from ribs of boats,
down to the dunes that curve
along the bay and arc the eye
out to a spit of shore, then, with a swerve,

still farther out, beyond
the current, churning water green to blue,
where a red buoy gongs its bell
and resonates. Oh, I can hear it, too,

Professor Pagels, look;
returning on the beach, that's me
precisely as I was,
poking a tentacled anemone,

while swift bank swallows whir
and swoop into their nesting holes
in colonies along the sandy cliffs,
and gulls dive in the shoals

squawking for broken crabs crushed in the tide.
The past is *now* wherever light
arrives in shifts of red
from galaxies whose distant flight

must be proportional
to the velocity at which they move away.
I see the boy's red pail;
I hear the buoy bell—as if that day

came back . . . but not to be possessed.
It comes back as the loss
of what it was—absence made palpable—
with all the glinting dross

of scallop shells and mandibles and claws
filling the foaming rush
of slushing tide along the shore—
without the grainy touch,

the suck of feet upon wet sand.
And now, in my own shifting sight, I feel
increasing distance from
my recollecting self, who seems unreal

to me—a me that's even
separated from the cliff here where I stand,
    my present life. Moving away
from that boy, swinging his bright, shell-filled pail,

    who hears a buoy bell
that long ago has ceased to ring,
moving away from the observer that I am
    this misted, swirling dawn, singing

    a red song to myself
among the flowing, windblown grass, I see
    my life arrive light-years from now,
complete, at someone else's galaxy.

Cosmic Recycling

As part of the cosmic recycling system, the solar wind dumps hundreds of millions of tons of solar material into outer space each second. By using artificial satellites that can move through the solar wind and transmit back data about its activity, scientists hear the creaks, groans, screams, thunderclaps, and drumrolls of our sun's song.

HEINZ R. PAGELS, *Perfect Symmetry*

Professor Pagels, somewhere in our galaxy
    evolved intelligence perhaps
considers us: "Earth's sun makes quite a racket
      with its creaks and thunderclaps,

like drumrolls imitating groans and screams."
    Though thousands of light-years away,
their data, more resolved than ours, tells them
    such groaning song is just the play

of solar wind recycling every second
    as it dumps solar material
in outer space. By sending satellites
    still closer to the mundane pull

      of our own atmosphere,
their instruments collect real human groans,
      real screams, rising in pitch,
    then softening to sobs and moans

like cellos under oboes, followed by
    a muted gasp, a pause.
    And from that measured silence now,
as if according to the cosmic laws

by which recycling must occur,
trilling of laughter—like a piccolo—
        floats in again and broadens
to the base guffaws of paired bassoons, which show

        that huffs and haws can be sustained
                a while in romping thirds
        until the mellowed next pause comes
from which new notes begin—like wooing birds.

        Amid the morning mist
the phoebe whistles her own name again;
        the dove prolongs her mournful call,
and soon shrill squawking of the busy wren,

        the warbling oriole, flurry
                the drowsy trees at noon;
the dipping swallows thrum the rafters of
        the shadowed barn, and then a loon,

                across the moonlit lake,
croons out his cry which echoes everywhere
        along the reedy coves until
the horned owl's round wail stuns the air.

        Beneath the sweep of solar wind,
the creaking sun, there's much variety
                to listen to on earth
        their distant scientists agree.

I wonder: would they hear it in sonata form
        with cycling thunderclaps and groans
accounted for—as if Mozart composed
        all anguish unsung in our bones?

Quasars

To get a feeling for the energy output of a quasar, imagine that a galaxy is the size of a room. A quasar would not be bigger than a barely visible speck of dust. Yet a single quasar produces 100 times the energy radiated by all the billions of stars in our galaxy. . . . And it radiates this energy for about 10 million years—a total amount equivalent to converting 100 million suns into pure energy.

HEINZ R. PAGELS, *Perfect Symmetry*

From wayward flight, I wake to dwell
upon my room—aswirl with dusty air—
a galaxy to call my own,
my cat curled like a comet in her chair.

Above the window sill, one speck,
at sudden dawn, floats brighter than the rest
as if a quasar glowed so purely
my mind's fevered quest

for consolation in the wish for worlds
born kinder than our own,
across expanding space-time's vast abyss,
returns me wistfully back home

to my own bed, my cat,
my musing eyes by which I see
a hundred million suns
in one lone speck of dust. It comforts me,

Professor Pagels, to imagine
light of such tremendous magnitude
scaled to my room so I can feel
Big Bang's leftover energy and brood

upon oblivion
of human hope and human grief:
the hope to have our little light remembered,
though unanswerably brief

compared to quasar radiation time;
the pain we cause—we fight
for territory to be buried in, we kill
as if death lasted for a night.

Framed by my window, maple branches bend
beneath the weight of wet, new snow
against a cloudless morning blue so clean,
so absolutely clear, I know

what cosmic beauty is in my own cells—
as if I understood
the firmament on God's fourth day
through holy eyes, and saw that *it was good*.

And yet the loveliness
of Mozart's Clarinet Quintet—darkly serene,
like circles on a lily pond
where one blue dragonfly alights—does seem

equally beautiful.
Praise to the human mind that rends
such fluid music out of silent dust,
out of itself, yet comprehends

its own minute place in the universe
as force flares out—goes on in waves,
in quantum leaps of light,
in galaxies emerging, autumn leaves

strewing their yellows on a lake,
or, on a winter dawn like this, as slow
        drops from the roof-hung icicles
shape clarinet notes, pausing on the snow.

        If we could cherish music
    in the dust, if only we could will
to love your light, receding quasar, we might live
    and die without the need to kill.

Brotherhood

Indeterminism implied the existence of physical events that were forever unknowable and unpredictable: when a particular atom is going to radiate or a particular nucleus undergo radioactive decay. Even God can give only the odds for some event to occur, not certainty. . . . Einstein remarked that he didn't believe God plays dice. . . . [But] the very act of attempting to establish determinism produces indeterminism. . . . Like us, God plays dice—He, too, knows only the odds.

H E I N Z R . P A G E L S , *The Cosmic Code*

"Vengeance is mine!" our angered Lord hath said.
It seems revenge sits well with Him,
and so I figure that the odds are good
He will forgive my whim,

my self-indulgence, if I contemplate
misfortune for my enemy
as unpreventable—
with stoic equanimity.

Another roll—the echoed knock of dice
against God's wall—and *zap*,
my nemesis, driving too fast, glances
perchance an instant at his map,

and, faithful to the law of Nature, hurtles
off the road into a tree.
Bearable grief is what I feel when news
of his conclusion reaches me.

Yet if he lived, he might
review my book this time with praise.
Weirdly, a God who gambles
works His vengeance in elusive ways,

for I now reconsider if
perhaps my foe were not so bad—I find
        an atom of regret
    is radiating in my mind;

I see remorse, now active in my heart,
        must have its solemn day.
    I feel diminished as I think
        he might have liked the way

    this epitaph imagines him
as generous enough to change his view
        of my subversive poems;
    he might have seen himself in you,

Professor Pagels, double of my double—
    indeterminate as my
blue evening shadow crossing over yours
        while we are pausing by

    the still shoal of a windless lake.
My grief is unpredictable, you see,
        and so I exercise the right
of thought: I take back my own fantasy

    in which his car swerves off the road,
collides against a tree, and snaps his head.
        He hits a ditch, rolls over twice;
he's cut, he's lost a tooth, but he's not dead.

    I've rescued him, not for divine
approval, but for Einstein's own sweet sake,
        to leave no stone unturned. The random
reason God plays dice is that He wants to break

connections tying action
to reward—that's how God sets us free
        to make peace with the odds.
Given another chance, my enemy

    climbs out the window of his car;
stunned by the light, he can't remember why
    he's there, or who he is. Red clouds,
warped in the lake, drift oddly in the sky.

Einstein

After 1926, Einstein . . . lost contact with the "old One" and his creative intuition. The delicate balance between innocence and experience, prerequisite for creativity, tipped toward experience. As [one] physicist said when he heard of Einstein's opposition to the new quantum theory, "We have lost our leader." Einstein held the classical view of determinism to the end of his life. For him, it was unthinkable that there was arbitrariness and chance in the fundamental structure of the universe.

H E I N Z R . P A G E L S, *The Cosmic Code*

Yes, one needs innocence to be
in contact with the "old One," hearing Him
assert His order in the image
of a burning bush. And cosmic whim

as arbitrary chance—
the fundamental structure of uncertainty
throughout the universe—that, too,
takes innocence to see,

like youthful Einstein's *"glücklichste Gedanke
meines Lebens,"* his life's happy fate
to think that an observer falling freely will
not feel his body's weight;

compared with other falling bodies, he'll
perceive himself to be at rest.
Like Moses humbled by amazing flames,
ecstatically possessed

by his Creator's *"I am that I am,"*
    Einstein envisions light that bends
in a straight line, since finite space is curved,
      and thus he comprehends

that gravitation is geometry.
      Oh, in holy wonder, *how*
all matter moves within a space-time warp
    reveals its law to him; he now

knows gravitation is equivalent
    to increased motion: where we live,
our restless place of earthly rest, our home,
    and where we go, are relative.

Newtonian experience, he still insists,
    shows all events must have a cause,
      and so the "old One" turns
away from His own chosen son; in that dim pause

    the age of randomness is born.
      The "old One" shakes His head,
while at the quantum border of uncertainty—
    "We've lost our leader," someone said.

      Barred from the promised land—
in which all forces might be unified
      within a single law—
    his strict faith held until he died;

he loved Mozartian serenity, and yet
    would not take morphine for his pain:
      "I want to go when *I* want . . ."
Einstein argued with the void. His eyes remain

a light to us—although
his nurse reported she had heard
but couldn't, at his deathbed, understand
his muttered, final German word.

Breaking

for Stanley and Virginia Bates

If we go back to the first moments of creation, the energy of the
primordial fireball was so high that the four interactions [gravity,
electromagnetism, weak force, strong force] were unified as one highly
symmetrical interaction. As this fireball of swirling quarks, colored
gluons, electrons, and photons expanded, the universe cooled and the
perfect symmetry began to break.

HEINZ R. PAGELS, *The Cosmic Code*

I conjure Einstein by the shore;
he stares at sunlight shimmering the sea—
a tiger shaking out its fur.
His heart still aches for the lost symmetry

of quarks primordial,
the interacting fireball, unified
within its simplifying flames,
before cooling expansion had divided

particles, divided night
from planetary day,
sundering matter in the process of
evolving life. The only way

the universe could make a conscious man
required the fireball's "thought"
of breaking symmetry, although desire
to reconcile all forces brought

torn Einstein to his grave
aghast. His life's wish to return
to a resolvable
simplicity had made his lamb's heart yearn

for solace from the "old One"—
order not allowing random chance.
    He saw the spume-limbed tiger flare
into a trillion lights, a fearful dance

    of sinewed forms and anvil sparks
        evolving toward no end
    even the "old One" could foresee,
as if the heedless universe must spend

    its whirling force in plenitude
        with no controlling hand,
merely unlikely laws of likelihood,
    which Einstein's mind can't understand.

        Big Bang, ex nihilo,
    oh tiger, tiger, burning bright,
of colored gluons, photons, swirling quarks,
    oh ocean of expanding light,

what arbitrary hand of chance dare break
        thy perfect symmetry?
Dazzle of starlight curved across the dome
    of Einstein's brain, bewilders me;

rebelling against randomness, he was
        determined not to see how such
chance breaking spoke the name of God. How could
        one mind conceive so much

yet yearn for more? Albert, rest your belovéd head
        by star-speared William Blake,
who scanned the heavens for God's grieving tears,
    grasping at light for the lamb's sake.

Mozart

Einstein loved the music of Mozart. Both these men shared the sense of the ultimate vulnerability of all life but never lost their sense of play or a ready laugh. They knew that in this world the reality of life is that it need not be. . . . [Einstein wrote that] "People who believe in physics know that the distinction between past, present, and future is only a stubbornly persistent illusion."

HEINZ R. PAGELS, *The Cosmic Code*

But once what *need not be* already *is,*
    laughter and music must
inevitably follow, like the laws
    that govern light, that bring from dust

      contending life, desire
to be alive, the will to make
some meaning flourish in the face of death,
      not merely for the sake

    of self, but for aspiring children
who come strutting after. Mozart, not
    Mozartian serenity,
lies spurned, dishonored in a pauper's grave to rot

    back to his silent elements.
      But listen: everywhere
beyond our lives, laughter of angels circles
      in the twilight air,

returning softly in sonata form.
    With thought resolved, the angels speak
wholly through Mozart's melodies, choraling
      cheek to breath-filled cheek,

except for one pipe-smoking angel
in a rumpled sweatshirt which declared
    in brazen rainbow colors that
        $E=mc^2$.

    Still sullen that in life he failed,
despite the constancy of light, to find
        a formula to unify
the forces in the universe, his mind,

            he sits off by himself—
reflecting on a corner cloud
why time is an illusion we cannot escape,
            too needful, and too proud

to know how fabricated our life is—
    until a large-nosed angel flies
            down to his heavy cloud,
    observing him with bulbous eyes:

"I've brought my piano, now forget yourself,
        let harmony begin!"
The wild-haired, rumpled angel brightens
        as he tunes his violin;

the large-nosed angel farts—and "Ah,"
        he cries, "it is decreed,
let music follow in the key of A!"
        Divinity unfolds, indeed,

from noisome gas to soaring aria,
        extolling matter yet
to be transcended, celebrating flesh
        whose brief enjoyment does beget

perfection of a kind: past, present, future—all
notes blend in the pure way
true laughing form unites them, first and last.
And now, by God, they play, they play!

Out of Nothing

The answer to the question "Where did the universe come from?" is that it came out of the vacuum. The entire universe is a reexpression of sheer nothingness. . . . If you add up all the energy in the universe it almost adds up to zero. [On the negative side] there is the potential energy of the gravitational attraction of the various galaxies for each other. . . . On the positive side of the ledger is the mass energy of all the particles in the universe. . . . If the two numbers matched, the total energy of the universe would be zero, and it wouldn't take any energy to create the universe.

HEINZ R. PAGELS, *The Cosmic Code*

That's good to hear, Professor Pagels, now
    that I feel so fatigued,
  so emptied out by husbanding
    and fathering, beleaguered

by the pleading needs of family and friends
    I need to care about, although
      it takes more summoned will
    each day not to let caring go

      back to the vacuum
  out of which it came, that equipoise
of numbers matched at zero energy—
    silent, without the noise

of hissing cosmic dust, vibrating stars
    that groan in drumroll thunderclaps.
My peace, eased free of consciousness, would be
    old zero's gift, and yet, perhaps

aware of universal nothingness, my self
            might still exist somehow
      by knowing that no self is there.
Since multiplying zero does allow

            a vacuum to create,
perhaps my own unbodied mind might be
      the lilting, melancholy, movement
            of a Mozart symphony

            expounding on a minor chord
until blank nothingness becomes a flute run
      balanced by a violin's reply.
            Selfless at last—un-

burdened back to careless rest, back to the void
            of undivided night,
the symmetry before, ex nihilo, the Big Bang,
      like Jehovah's cry, "Let there be light!"

            began the prayer of mind
in lamentation to return to dust,
      to particles, to primal
zero, our first home—would I then know the thrust

      of nothing to express itself,
creating matter and creating space,
      as if I were a messenger
of cosmic absence, yes, as if my human face

            were destined to appear,
      and after me, my children, too—
            with space inventing time?
But now, Professor Pagels, brother, you,

compounded double of myself,
appear reposing in exhaustion of your own
          with bare November nearing
as, reflected blazing on a lakefront stone

          your unborn son will step upon,
sweetness of evening light leaps up, and, yes,
          you feel the surging countersweet
                of sheerest emptiness.

The Black Hole

Imagine [that] the whole mass of the sun is crushed down to a radius of a few kilometers. The gravity and space curvature near this compacted sun is enormous. . . . Since light cannot leave this object, it "appears" as a black hole in space. . . . An observer who fell into the center of a black hole could see time slow down. But the falling observer can never communicate his strange experience to his friend outside.

HEINZ R. PAGELS, *Perfect Symmetry*

My brother and I planned to meet
at our secluded campsite up in Maine
       beside an azure lake
swarming with rainbow trout. I'd hired a local plane

    to fly me to our dock, but when
I saw how beaten up it was, how queerly
      the old pilot squinted upwind
at the sun, I felt a fleeting shock of fear.

    A reject of the Wright Brothers?
Or had he built it with his son—sort of
      a modern Daedalus?
Its banged pontoons were dented right above

    the waterline which seemed to me
too high for the sad bird to lift its ass
      for takeoff. But, by God,
it did! The pilot made, I thought, a needless pass

      between two quarry walls,
    then brushed the treetops just to show
      where a tornado scythed
a highway through the woods, ten years ago,

which wound back on itself.
When we arrived, my waiting brother waved his hands
    wildly from the dock's edge.
The pilot asked, "How's 'bout before we land

      we do a couple lucky loops?"
      The first loop made me squeeze
my thighs against my groin, and with the second,
    wider loop, the engine wheezed,

shuddered, and stopped. We slid into a nose dive,
    spinning toward the evening sun
reflected in the lake. Oh, I was falling
    through my mind's black hole, the one

      curved space to float me home,
so slowly I had time to think that I
    alone had nothing left to know
except the circle of the sun within the sky

    inside the water, blue advancing
      bluer into brighter blue—
although my unbelieving brother held his hands
    over his face. And you,

Professor Pagels, would you not have seen,
      reflected in my eyes,
the unresisted pull into the perfect heart
    of orange light, the last surprise

of pure acceptance that can never pass
      beyond itself? I guess
    the gas ran back into the engine,
      for we leveled out, and, yes,

terror returned the instant we touched down,
        and my taut body knew
that I was safe there in my brother's arms.
        Next morning my whole chest was bruised

where I had clutched myself, and one week later,
        back in the old river town
by the abandoned mill, we learned my pilot's plane
        had crashed in the dense mountain

flying home. "Don't know how Joel lasted
        long's he did," his neighbor said.
We sat, a covenant of brothers by the fire,
        and yet the orange-red,

the green-blue flames distracted me; I watched
        the sizzling rainbow trout that night,
its smeared red stripe surrounded by black dots—
        collapsed suns lost in their trapped light.

Number

The nothingness "before" the creation of the universe is the most complete void that we can imagine—no space, time, or matter existed. It is a world without place, without duration or eternity, without number ... Yet this unthinkable void converts itself into the plenum of existence—a necessary consequence of physical laws. Where are these laws written into the void? What "tells" the void that it is pregnant with a possible universe?

H E I N Z   R.   P A G E L S, *Perfect Symmetry*

Mothering void, ripe emptiness,
      pregnant with number—*one*,
the number first of all for the duration
    each of us enjoys beneath the sun,

our single sun, and yet a minor star among
    such billions in the Milky Way,
      I thank you for one lifetime
    being what I am before the day

I separate into more stable particles.
      Thanks, equally, for *two*,
the other by which one conceives oneself as one,
      apart, and yet a part of you,

Oh void unthinkable, your child of place—
      this cooling quantum mess
of hydrogen and helium, of chairs and cats,
    your unknown law of nothingness

converted to the plenum of existence like
    the animals from Noah's ark
who clump the ramp boards, bumping on their way
    where light breaks through the fertile dark.

We two together now in thought,
Professor Pagels, let's give thanks to *three*—
perhaps three apples in a bowl,
or, in a cherry tree,

three calling birds whose random voices
blend within the mind
and on their branches make a triangle
should I elect to find

a pattern there. To meet my need,
another bird alights,
an oriole, and lo! a rectangle appears,
as through the summer nights

the constellation, Leo Minor, guards
my dreaming house, accompanied
by five-starred Lyra's harp chords in the wind
while multiplying numbers breed

their imaged offspring in the womb of sleep.
So I recite myself among
the stars, the crystal hexagons of snow,
electrons, protons—each one sung

for its own numbered self to celebrate
possible matter, time, and space,
including me to think of the unthinkable,
to give the pregnant void a face

(only a while, a nanosecond measured
even by our finite sun)
yet long enough to call her *Mother*, long enough to count
from zero up to number one.

Leftover Laughter

Researchers found that the black empty space of the universe was not absolutely cold; it has a slight temperature of three degrees Kelvin above absolute zero. This temperature is due to a radiation bath of photons that permeates all of space. . . . The interpretation of this radiation bath is that it is heat left over from the Big Bang.

HEINZ R. PAGELS, *The Cosmic Code*

I am consoled! There's energy enough
          to bathe black, empty space
with photons still left over from the flash
          that shimmered on our mother's face—

the patient void—when fathering Big Bang
          let loose his mighty, first guffaw
          to fill the universe
          and sow the quintessential law

          of laughter, consciousness
is gifted to enjoy: that matter should
          (including us) exist at all,
should be, and go on going on for good

          or ill, for better or for worse.
But that gargantuan guffaw, awesome
          in its orgasmic,
          fecundating thrust, its kingdom come,

          was just part sneeze, propelled
from brooding Big Bang's tickled nose, part blast
          of belch, part flare of flatulence,
cacophony of quarks, until, at last,

the universe as body, mass
as energy and energy as mass, became
        transformed to spirit when, through us,
originating laughter found a name

        for everything that *is*
and flourished into breathful form.
So, Adam, playing his first game, identified
        the animals—the cold and warm,

the high and low, fins slicing through the sea,
                bright plumage of the air,
        beasts of the field—according to
their species' attributes, while taking care

        to note each differentiation,
kind from kind: *aardvark*—an awkward sound
                to fit his awkward ears;
the *hippopotamus* for her repeating round

        of heavy syllables
and splashing *p*s; *mosquito* for his light,
        staccato-like attack (although
zanzara in Italian with its blight

        of buzzings zeroed in
also appealed to Adam, polyglot);
        and *squirrel*, her *r*s scampering
                over mossed rocks on hot

September afternoons to counterpoint
        the *pileated woodpecker*
                whose crisp, percussive knocks
upon the hollowed hemlock trunk all blur

and fade downwind along the stream;
then, finally, the *duckbilled platypus*
   to indicate unlikely luck—
pure pleasure of the perfectly preposterous,

   leftover laughter from Big Bang!
And later melancholy Adam loved to tilt
   their leaping names on his quick tongue,
     to feel the push and lilt

of vowels on his lips, when, two by two,
     they disappeared from sight.
He missed their moving presence and their touch,
     and by his fire at night

he'd speak their names out loud for company
   and scan the laughing dark to find
them safely there, just as, Professor Pagels, now,
   I summon your warm words to mind.

The First Word at Last

This sense of the unfathomable beautiful ocean of existence drew me into science. I am awed by the universe, puzzled by it and sometimes angry at a natural order that brings such pain and suffering. Yet any emotion I have toward the cosmos seems to be reciprocated by neither benevolence nor hostility but just by silence.

HEINZ R. PAGELS, *Perfect Symmetry*

From me, Professor Pagels, it's
reciprocation that you get, though I've delayed
    meeting you in person
until our fictive friendship had been played

    out on our cosmic stage
with a fine flourish. Ah, in your awed way
    you've praised unfathomable beauty
in the universe which, as you say

    most poignantly, responds
with icy silence to our suffering.
    And so I've tried to compensate
with stanzas in adversity to sing

    to you, day into night,
as father, brother, son, always as friend—
    preceding me, surviving me,
from the Big Bang beginning to the end—

    companion as the scanning double
of my self-regarding self. Out of the slime,
    into the trees, across the stars
in mental flight, as if annihilating time

can be contained in thought,
through microspace and macrospace,
through windfall, snowfall, mist, and rain, I see
existence as a face

that I can gaze upon and love, a voice
that says: *Be fruitful, multiply*—
except for pain we humans cause, except for flesh
that does not choose to die.

I sit here on a rock, the spent tide's bright foam
at my feet, and stare out at the sea
at dawn, almost serene,
as if bred for eternity,

as if conceiving beauty—consciousness
of its own self through human eyes—
was what the universe
first started out to realize

as possible: number from nothingness,
sandpipers scampering at noon
thin-legged along the blazing beach. Chasing the waves,
they disappear too soon

for me to count them—oh, but surely
they were there! I still can picture how
their wing stripes spilled the light;
I hear their *twick* cries quickened even now

as if forever I might hold them
vivid in my mind,
but not as answer, not as anything
that I can use to find

meaning in extinction back to nothingness. No,
        heartbreaking beauty must suffice—
the brotherhood of sharing what we lose,
            the rainbow in warmed ice.

Let there be emptiness to fill and let
        the universe be silent, though,
tomorrow, Heinz—yes, you can count on it—
            I'll call to say *hello*.

Outlasting You

Dr. Heinz R. Pagels, an experienced climber, fell to his death from a peak in Colorado on July 24, 1988, at the age of 49. At the conclusion of The Cosmic Code *he had written: "I dreamed I was clutching at the face of a rock but it would not hold. Gravel gave way. I grasped for a shrub, but it pulled loose, and in cold terror I fell into the abyss. Suddenly . . . I realized that what I embody, the principle of life, cannot be destroyed. It is written into the cosmic code, the order of the universe. As I continued to fall in the dark void, embraced by the vault of the heavens, I sang to the beauty of the stars and made my peace with the darkness."*

And now, unfathomably soon,
dear Heinz, a first *good-bye*; I had not dreamed
I would endure outlasting you.
    I wonder if it seemed,

in that suspended interval,
    though still obedient
to cosmic laws, you had outlived
your final fears because somehow you meant

to choose your accident amid
    such stony randomness
and thus keep true a wide-eyed vow to live
    in touch with your abyss—

darkness encoded in the vault
    of your reflecting mind.
Dwelling on your own corresponding stars,
    you had rehearsed your death to find

the right last thought that might
contain eternity: the gravel giving way,
the grasping for a prickly shrub—
its snug roots, pallid gray,

suddenly naked in the sun.
And then, before acceleration starts,
as if the air will hold
your body up, there's time to feel your heart

push forth a surge of blood;
there's time to feel a gasp leap out,
expanding from your lungs,
a cringing whisper first, and then a shout,

embodied as a scream.
A *No!* a full, involuntary *No!*
unwinds as if from someone else,
another life below,

preceding yours, your father's cry,
a stranger's, or perhaps
you hear my decomposing voice
come echoing unloosed from a crevasse.

Descending with my arms outstretched—
my knees like twin moons orbiting my head—
through my own galaxy,
a shrub uprooted from its gravel bed

like a commanding scepter
in my hand, I try deliberately now
to dream your liberating dream
of the encompassing abyss, of how,

at last, you sang out to the stars.
Though soon, my friend, it will not matter who
                preceded whom, tonight
        at home I cannot follow you

                unfathomably light
in thought embracing the indifferent air.
        With my grief's *No* upon my lips,
appalled because you summoned me to dare

        to make peace with the dark that lasts
                so everlasting long,
I'm earthbound with *good-bye*, but bless you for
        the starlit beauty of your song.

About the Author

Robert Pack has taught for twenty-five years at Middlebury College, where he is the Donald E. Axinn Professor of Literature and Creative Writing and Director of the Bread Loaf Writers' Conference. His books of poetry include *The Irony of Joy; A Stranger's Privilege; Guarded by Women; Home from the Cemetery; Nothing but Light; Keeping Watch; Waking to My Name; Faces in a Single Tree* (Godine, 1984); and *Clayfeld Rejoices, Clayfeld Laments* (Godine, 1987). Pack lives in a valley by the Green Mountains in Cornwall, Vermont.

BEFORE IT VANISHES

was set in Galliard by DEKR Corporation, Woburn, Massachusetts. Designed by Matthew Carter and introduced in 1978 by the Mergenthaler Linotype Company, Galliard is based on a type made by Robert Granjon in the sixteenth century, and is the first of its genre to be designed exclusively for photo-typesetting. A type of solid weight, Galliard possesses the authentic sparkle that is lacking in the current Garamonds. The italic is particularly felicitous and reaches back to the feeling of the chancery style, from which Claude Garamond in his italic had departed.

The book was designed by Lucinda Hitchcock. It has been printed and bound by Haddon Craftsmen, Scranton, Pennsylvania.